Perlita   Deace

FEMINISM

THE

DRIVING FORCE

NO ONE WAS BORN A FEMINIST

WE WERE DRIVEN TO BECOME ONE...IT IS NOT A FIGHT AGAINST MEN...

WE ALL SHOULD BE FEMINIST

INTRODUCTION

There have been a lot of misconceptions surrounding feminism, and over the past decades, such misconceptions are yet to be abated. The divergence of opinion and motives of promoters of the movement in some cases have in no small measure contributed to misapprehensions of the original intention of the movement.

Various researches have been carried out by academics and a host of other writers, have written on various topics related to feminism but none have really thrown light into what will suddenly make a man or a woman become a feminist what will make a known introvert suddenly rise up through the barriers of his/her personality traits to the forefront of speaking up for women, men or the voiceless girl child.

In 'Feminist-The driving force' we looked into that which is responsible for driving both men and women into this noble course from a personal experience and perspective and from the experience of few others.

It began with an overview of what feminism is about its definition and the concept of force or drive as internal energy which propels everyone to stand up in what they believe.

Then followed by my personal experience right from home growing up followed my experiences, in the university, in politics, and later in my place of work. My experiences were corroborated with other men and women who in one way or the other have had their own life experiences which triggered the drive in them to speak for humanity.

Some have argued that feminists and feminism as a movement is an all-out war with men, but that is not correct. The next chapter attempts to show that it is not about women fighting men or attempting to leave their place to take the place of men but that both sexes are victims and as humans deserve equal human rights.

Feminism is about the protection of rights for all humans with the main focus on women and the girl child who are the major victims. It is a just cause pushing for a deserved dignity for all gender irrespective of their age.

The final chapter emphasizes the need for all persons men and women, all human rights advocate seeing feminism as a right course geared towards the protection of human dignity and the need to raise and support, lend their voices to end human rights abuses as pertains to gender inequality.

CHAPTER ONE

OVERVIEW OF FEMINISM

WHAT IS FEMINISM?

Feminism can be defined as a subset of the human rights movements geared toward defining establishing, equal political rights, monetary compensation, social rights, and the provision of equal opportunities for women. Upon this definition was the original movement of social activists advocating for women's rights founded and named. However, this definition has since been expanded to capture all genders whose rights are also affected. The new definition of FEMINISM according to Gender Equality Institute is; a collective term used to describe social and political movements that seek to question the inequality that exists between men and women.

It is an idea that borders on women's privileges. Feminism is predominantly centered on issues related to the female gender, but since feminism looks for gender rights balance, a few women activists contend that men's freedom is in this way an essential piece of feminism and that men are likewise hurt by sexism and gender-sensitive job opportunities.

The expanded concept of feminism advocates for social, political, monetary, and scholarly equity for both women and men.

Feminism is an honorable idea and concept against reprehensible segregation on the grounds of gender. In the beginning, the division of sex jobs depended on the ability to bear and support children and make provision available for the family the whole time. The division had no contention for centuries but was later on contested less intensely and now strongly. This might be as a result of the male gender taking their jobs all the more seriously and consciously or unconsciously subverting female jobs by refuting them totally in the entire scheme of things. The origin of this violation and suppression may be related to Men's actual strength, their capacity to chase (maybe the money for instance), and their being independent of the responsibility of childbearing made them high-headed and haughty towards the female. Under this setting, we can see the making of a man-centric culture where all normal practices were made and constrained by men, while women were largely uninvolved accomplices in the entire course.

Feminism is the promotion of an ideology that is beyond women's privileges on the grounds of equity of genders. It started in the west, displayed all through the world, and was exemplified by countless individuals and foundations resolved to activity on conviction of women's privileges and interests. According to Dr. Susan Currie Sivekit, feminism is a social movement seeking equality for all gender with an emphasis on the need for people to be able to chase any opportunity regardless of gender.

WHO IS A FEMINIST?

Many have continued to misunderstand the true meaning of the word 'Feminist'. They have largely related to it as a group of women speaking for women's rights. But this is just part of the whole truth. It is a word that at first will trigger a negative impression about a female gender engaging in some kind of social war with men in an attempt to put the male gender down. The Cambridge dictionary defines a feminist as one who believes in feminism and one who supports any change that will help the female gender to have equal treatment and opportunity like the male gender. This definition in no small way has contributed to the negative notion upon which our society sees feminists. The definition limits the interest of feminists to only the female gender, which is untrue because feminism stands for all gender according to Dr. Susan Currie Sivek. Although it is a movement that started first because of women, it has since expanded to include all gender.

CHAPTER TWO

DRIVE – A MOTIVATING FORCE

Nothing just happens! There's always a trigger. In physics, according to Isaac Newton's first law of motion, 'a body will remain in its state of rest or motion unless it was acted upon by an external force'. The word 'body' as used in the law of motion can be likened to be a belief system, an idea, assumption, or situation. This accepted belief or idea will remain until someone questions its acceptability. The drive is the internal trigger that propels every activist to pursue a course they believe is right.

The 'Drive' concept may very well be alluded to as an internal inward inspiration or motivation to arrive at a specific goal or task. Agreeing with T.Stuart Watson et al in their book 'encyclopedia of the school of psychology, there are two types of drives; primary or essential and auxiliary or secondary drives. Essential drives are straightforwardly identified with ones need for survival and it is connected to very basic human needs such as food, water, and oxygen. Auxiliary or secondary drives are those that are socially decided or learned, for example, the drive to acquire money, closeness, or social endorsement. The driving hypothesis holds that these drives persuade individuals to prioritize their needs by choosing to respond to that which will help them to achieve the goal. For instance, when an individual feels hungry, the person in question is persuaded to lessen that drive by eating; when there is a job needing to be done, the individual is propelled to finish it.

Forces, like, convictions, values, interests, and noble courses can spur individuals. Apart from these powers or forces, for example, belief, interests, and convictions are internal motivating factors. Others are external, for example, risk, the climate, or pressing factors from a friend or family member. Drives are accepted to begin inside an individual and may not need outer improvements to have an effect.

CHAPTER THREE

KNOWLEDGE AND EXPEREINCE ARE THE DRIVING FORCE FOR FEMINISM

A PERSONAL EXPERIENCE

I grew up as the only female child with two brothers. My elder brother would do most of the home chores when I was younger but at the age of seven, I noticed I was left to handle what he used to do and even my twin brother like my elder, are well exempted and given a more of freedom that I don't get. As we grew older, things even got worse, they will eat and won't wash the dishes if or decide to do it whenever they feel like it and no one questions them. When mum finds out that the kitchen is dirty and untidy she blames me irrespective of who had used the dishes. They will hardly sweep the sitting room. Whenever mum was cooking I must be the one to work with her while my brothers are having fun playing games or something else for fun. I had never liked this sense of oppression and inequality I experience as a child right in my own house. On several occasions, I have questioned my mum why I am being treated this way and her short responses in most cases are 'you are a woman or they are boys'. As I grew older, I realized that this is not going to go away, the unfair treatment is what I have to accept, move on, and someday in the future, pass it on to my daughters as well as an accepted culture. It evolved to the point where I had to dish their food and serve them at the dining. If I didn't bring the food to the dining sometimes, I will hear statements like this from them, 'are you sure you will be a good wife? Is this how you will treat your husband? Don't you understand this is a learning opportunity for you?? And the list of questions goes on. Occasionally I questioned my mum severally about how I felt in my house and how unfair I am being treated. In some cases, her response would be "don't you know you are a woman"? At that time, I didn't fully grasp what she really meant. But one thing was dawning on me; women are more of the second class whose opinion didn't really count.

My dad is a wonderful father but I don't think I would consider him as a wonderful husband. He may not have physically attacked my mum at least I can't recall, but the way he talks to her at times is so harsh and shows a lack of respect. Then as I grew older I observed that this was a common attribute of most men from his clan, and every man is expected to be an active lord and commander in chief over his wife. This accepted culture made me vow never to get married to a man from my father's clan.

Before I ever came to know the word 'feminism or feminist', a part of me was yearning for a fairer treatment first between me and my brothers and for men and women. My childhood experience activated a consciousness of inequality from home to my society.

I began to clearly see a pattern that is deeply rooted in the society and it became as though no one was saying anything about it. I became very conscious of gender inequality that was manifesting itself in different areas of our society.

In university, I was very outspoken and the class head in my department. I desired to be our faculty representative, an elective post that is fiercely contested and dominated mainly by male students. When I indicated interest to contest for the office, I was clearly informed that the office available to females was the assistant representative position. This information didn't come to me as a shock. However, as appalled as I was, I pushed forward toward the vision. Unfortunately, I didn't get enough votes to qualify for the real election. I may link this to gender inequality as the majority of the executive members (who will vote in the primary election) are men and the thought of having a woman head and give instruction to them didn't go well with most of them. So right from the primary level, they made sure I didn't qualify to contest for the presidential post.

I worked in the banking industry for over fifteen years and rose to the position of branch manager in one of the biggest banks in my country. We had a good number of female managers across the nation and so one would expect a good level of equality across the board (so I thought) until I got a shocker.

We had an audit exercise that requires verification of staff database and it required interfacing with the human resources department. A colleague of mine in another branch who works in the human resources department received the wrong database of staff from what she was supposed to get. She observed something shocking and appalling as she went through the data. She came across my name and observed that my salary was 15.8 percent less than my male colleagues in the same categories as me and even some men with less experience than I am are earning higher. I was saddened by this development and I wrote to my boss of my intention to resign if the issue of salary disparity is not addressed. After presenting the evidence to them, eventually, my salary was scaled up. This is not just happening to me alone, but the countless number of other women in the company who are not bold enough to speak or are not aware at all. Nine months later, I resigned when I got a better offer elsewhere.

OTHER FEMINISTS' EXPERIENCE

The account of individuals who have either had a personal experience or the experience of someone close to them which inspired them to support feminism and human rights in general are presented below. Some of the names of these testifiers have been changed as they requested but their stories are all valid.

KAYAM

In my family, I have five siblings; four sisters and a brother. I recollect my mom making an effort not to take her little girls to be cut. My mom felt weak battling against a custom that has been around and practiced for more than five centuries.

I was ten years of age when I was sent for circumcision. A neighbor took me to a house owned by the oldest lady in our community. She was notable for being a gift to girls they said. In Uganda, we didn't have appropriate centers for these systems. We didn't have specialists in white coats and gloves. We didn't have sedation to numb the pains that comes with the procedures. There are nearly zero hygiene practices adopted in her cutting procedures, the woman who cut us utilized a sharp blade; blood flickering on its edge. She used a similar blade on all the young ladies.

Inside her home, were numerous young ladies who had been sent from the different villages across the communities. None of us knew one another, however, the vast majority of us realized we were there for a similar reason. There were four senior ladies praising and singing tunes, bringing young ladies, individually, to the back room. Their voices rose to become dim to the sound of excruciating shouts. As I sat, standing by, young ladies returned, agonizingly crying as blood streamed down their legs. They could scarcely walk. The ball was in my court.

As the ladies came to bring me, I started to battle with them. I would not like to experience this. Two ladies snatched me by my arms and another two by my legs. They constrained my back to the table and kept on holding me down with such strength. The lady with the blade took a glance at me and stated, "The more you struggle with us, the more it will hurt. The cutting will happen quickly in the event that you relax."

I actually feel that pain. You feel it in every last bit of your body. I saw a lot of blood that I've never seen before. I thought I was dying. It was finished. I wailed and I cried. The ladies started to sing their tunes, saluting me on turning into an unadulterated lady. They said I had acquired my pride.

When it was time for me to get married at an 'accepted age', I was removed from school, in the wake of finishing just four years of my schooling. Female education was considered irrelevant and less important than male child. They believe that the best security that can be offered to the girl child is to lead her into a marriage where she would be protected by the husband with the assurance of a better future. We were rather taught and trained on how to cook, clean, wash and general domestic work was of more importance than education.

I was fifteen when I was directed to the man that married me. I felt defenseless. By the grace of God, we were blessed with four children one boy and three girls.

We were living in Uganda when my oldest girl turned seven. when it was time for her to attended to. Similarly, like my mom, I was unable to bear the prospect of getting my young daughters to go through this and the chance of losing one forever. For what reason would it be for me to have my girls go through the torment and agonizing pain I experienced? Why would I have to put their life at risk knowing full well the potential of death coming to them if they go through the procedure?

I purposed in my heart to save and protect the lives of my daughters while we still live in my country. I understand that as long as we still live here, one day the elders in my family will take my daughters to be cut without my consent or knowledge. Now, this fight is bigger than my family. And I don't know how long I would continue to battle an established cultural practice that is beyond my family and we could be banished from the community and this will bring a bigger shame to my immediate and extended family.

TAMARA

In our culture, every lady that has attained the minimum age of marriage accepted by our people which is usually at the age of eighteen will have to go through 'exercise' before her marriage. In my home, when my sister attained the age and the time came for her to embark on the journey alongside other ladies, the woman responsible for taking the young ladies came very early in the morning and took my sister away to the town where it will be done.

After some time, one of the elderly women who deal with the activities went to our home and said that there were a few complications as a result of the operation for my sister.

Several young women came back to the town to join the bam bam. In our community, an extraction is an event that usually calls for big celebrations, and it requires no financial commitment from the parents and family of the lady, the young lady is guaranteed to wed. At night, my sister was conveyed, back to our home, sick. We called the medication man who attempted to bring to an end the excess bleeding she had been going through all day. The bleeding continued all night, the effort of the medicine man did not really improve her situation. The news had been passed around in the town and everyone was in a sober mood, and because she was the eldest among her set that did the operation, there was no celebration. After over a day of excruciating pain and bleeding and agony, she passed on the next day.

My mum, who had lost her seventh child, was devastated and fainted. She was going to commit suicide and end it all. We had to put her under special care and monitoring for months for her to be strong and get herself back again after the tragic loss of her daughter.

The information on my sister's demise spread throughout the other villages and towns around. Not because this was the first unfortunate case, but in the light of the fact that my dad was a popular chief in our town. This custom of ours which some time ago was a significant event for individuals to show their abundance and societal position – has lost its popularity in the whole region. Different young ladies had lost their lives from extraction before my sister but because of the status of my dad and on the grounds that my sister was so popular, her unfortunate and pointless passing caused the individuals in the entire region to be aware of the risk. I and other women embarked on a massive campaign against this custom and the need to allow the girl child to live her life without being forced against her will and her right trampled upon because of some unhealthy culture that has no relevance in human and woman living in particular.

Although this custom has become very unpopular over the years, some very few families do engage in it and the unfortunate death from the exercise is still being reported occasionally.

DAN

I'm really very good with facial make-up as a makeup artist, but when I applied for this make-up job as a young guy, I was told that I cannot be accepted. That the role is only for females, despite the fact that they were much slower, less creative and I did better than all in the fitness tests. The same applied for a receptionist job opening I applied for, after passing the test with the right skill set, I was also turned down simply because I am not a female, the preferred individual should have a female tone they said.

Fast forward, I was permitted to be a worker, to work on a homestead or on the rail routes. That is the place where men work. It is very interesting to note that, they'd let me work where I had no skill set, yet they wouldn't allow me to work where I had abilities. They gave me the fitness test to avoid me, and when they discovered I was in the top percentile, they rejected me.

At a point when my three young kids were in school, their stepmother who is my partner decided to get a low-hour job. How cool, I thought. How long? (I asked) she said 'around three days a week'. Wonderful I thought. Maybe I could work three days too, and we'd get more wages and some good tax cuts too. But I was shocked at her response. 'Never going to happen she said. You are living in a dream world on the off chance that you believe I'm returning to work so you can cut your hours!' Geez, this did not go well with me at all, this is not what the feminism I have stood for and cherished is about. You know, the aim and goal of feminism as I know it, is about fairness for the two sexes.

I was having a private instructional course with a female student on the most proficient method to utilize guitar and other melodic instruments and this is after regular school class in a homeroom in a region where individuals strolled and pass by frequently. I personally picked the space. A female colleague then came and opened the entryway and put a wedge in it to hold the entryway open, I was mad at her action. To her all men are dangerous.

It was at this point it dawned on me that the course and mission of the movement may have been hijacked by some women, things had changed. I have always been an ardent supporter of feminism because of the fact that I thought that the world was unmistakably not balanced, yet when it came time for fairness for me, I discovered it was about 'decisions for ladies' ... not equity for all.

LISA

My story began in the Philippines when I was in secondary school. I come from a low-pay average earning family where we were not lacking any dinners or fundamental solace, yet there was no abundance of extravagance as well. I was raised by my mother, who has been an extraordinary motivation and inspiration in my life.

I generally got the best grades in school and was extraordinary at math. I had never really thought about the possibility that as I am a female, certain callings were "manly" until, at the youthful age of fourteen. So one day I told my mum, of my choice to study engineering in the presence of her cousin, my aunt. To my greatest surprise my aunt interjected and asked "Why not become a secretary and study public administration? That it is more appropriate for a young lady like you, and may be your boss will like you and decide to marry you.

I was furious, her suggestions and remarks didn't sound good to me by any means! Why should I live my life depending on the day a man will see and marry me before I can live my dream life? For what reason wouldn't I be able to become an engineer but to turn into a secretary? From that day, I vowed and promised them I would go for my dream field of study, engineering, and I would make a lot of fortune enough to support any man I choose to marry if he is not as rich as I am. It was to me an official announcement and declaration of battle against an accepted average mindset by many women in my community, I will rather remain unmarried and live this dream out.

TINA

I moved to Sweden in 2011 and I decided for the first time in my life to venture into business. Being a migrant here, and not knowing many individuals, someone acquainted me with a top personnel in the African American population community. After several appointments with him, it was clear how he anticipated I should show my appreciation; with a touch on the knee, his hand on my leg. To state that it was a nauseating experience will be an understatement. It was a mixture of anger and frustration.

I didn't inform anyone about it at that time. He was a particularly known figure, who will believe me if I raise my concern and travails? I only decided to step back and pulled out from everything. It's another obstacle for ladies, particularly ladies of color—how sad it could be? that in strange land where one would expect to find some solace in her community but instead it turned out to be a place where you can't trust or confide in any one from your community, where do one go from here?

As a real estate personnel, an opportunity came and I became a senior project manager for an International initiative geared towards helping Caribbean and Latin America. It is a field well dominated by men, some of the men that I worked with overlooked me when I raised some concerns or sent an email. I even hear some make statements like, "Are you certain she can accomplish the work?" or "See her, see physical statue... There happens to be a great deal about women's bodies here.

These kinds of experiences are common in the part of the world where I hail from, South America. However, in Sweden the issue was more of sexism. All these experiences and encounters from coworkers have a negative influence in one's creative ability towards the project before them. It impacts your capacity to be inventive which could help to improve the project. It became a complex working environment for me, considering the fact that I am black, a woman, and an immigrant. It is a daunting task to address all these vices daily.

My years in the real estate industry were filled with many stories and experiences, but at a point I decided it is time to step aside and focus on my personal business. Presently, in my work as a coach, I mentor a lot, most of my customers are racialized ladies. I show them how to stay away from what I considered think traps but instead, they should leverage more on their professional skills, through training and personal development and also stand up and speak not just for themselves but also for other women.

These are not new gender equality issues in organizations, and one of the easy and effective ways to address the issue is to first have diversity in the organizations' leadership representation.

Furthermore, organizations would see an ever increasing number of high-potential and well skilled individual representatives leaving, and this may not really be a direct result of compensation yet might be on the grounds that they don't feel respected, accepted or they're constantly confronting sexism and prejudice.

CHAPTER FOUR

MISCONCEPTION ABOUT FEMINISM

FEMINISM IS NOT ABOUT HATING MEN

Hatred for the male gender and being a feminist are totally different things. These days without knowing, just to oppose the idea, to act like a cool individual who doesn't follow the trends, some will profess to be feminists. Look, It is not an offense for not being a feminist, but one ought to in any event comprehend what it implies and what it speaks to. Without information, making wrong and uncivilized moves is an indication of stupidity, not knowledge. Anyone who advocates for the girl child to get the education of her choice has her right to reproduction decision, equivalent compensation for equivalent work, actively standing against sexual brutality, lending their voice against any form of deprivation of the female gender; you are a FEMINIST.

The demand by feminists is for balance equality whether it's in the workplace, school, clinic, or anywhere else. These days ladies are attempting to escape from the shadows of men and decide to work even when married. Few are censured at home, others face difficulty at the workplace. Ladies being unique compared to men have various necessities, not extraordinary but rather unique. For example, a recently married woman in some cultures may need a couple of days off to cultivate her day-to-day life and stun her in-laws, something which men do not need to make a fuss over. Also, if she gets pregnant, she would need to take additional consideration; she can't do weighty work, she maintains a strategic distance from all that which can cause the baby discomfort or lead to complicated health issues. And all these new changes will definitely impact her work performance at some point in her career for which she may be blasted for poor performance. Other natural activities like the menstrual cycle for some women may have a serious impact on them on monthly basis. It is worthy of note that women are not the same as men and so special consideration must be made with regards to their needs.

The fact is, men and women are different. For instance, they have diverse sexual organs and genetic makeup. Men have testosterone and more muscle tissues and physical toughness. We can also look at the sexual capability of both genders, what one can naturally do and the other unable to. The big question is why should all these natural features be the reasons to segregate and deprive someone in terms of their ability and talents? Why is it assumed that men will excel more in mathematics than women and so women are discouraged from studying it?

Society is so used to the objective of men, that they don't perceive that ladies' strength has different requirements. Again, because they are used to having only men around, they think one bunch of prerequisites, provisions, and rules mainly designed with men in mind can also be applied to women. Society fails to realize that even though this has been an accepted norm for a long time, it still doesn't make it right.

IT IS NOT A BATTLE OR CONTEST WITH MEN

There is no size fit all definition for feminism, it is diverse for everyone. It is simply a demand for a balance system that recognizes the rights of everyone. Equity in training, equity in democracy, equal privileges in open job positions, career advancements, and so on.

A feminist should not be seen as somebody who is attempting to remove or dethrone men, but someone who is demanding for what actually belongs to them. They need opportunity and freedom from men. They are not requesting that men love them, nor are they requesting unrivaled treatment, what's desired is consistency in every area of life. Nobody wishes to work in an unfriendly working condition, scared to remain out late, perceptually typified, or other numbers of issues that are frowned at by ladies' all around the globe. They simply need to be enabled to secure themselves, to do things in their terms, to be taught without segregation. They should be considered proficient as men can be, the existence of any form of segregation and restriction inhibits them from displaying their gifts. They do not wish to be considered based on their gender or appearance but for their characteristics and abilities and there isn't anything awkward about these demands.

Feminism demands a balance of rights between genders. It is important to comprehend the best treatment to be given, to bring the genders to a standard and not to make one gender have an edge over the other. This notion has caused numerous men to avoid the idea of feminism and all that it represents as a movement.

True feminists do not imply that men don't confront any issues or they are invulnerable to segregation and discrimination. Each issue centers on a specific topic and that is how feminists help women to address their issues. It is not as if some men don't face issues that women face (discrimination based on gender) but because we have more advocacy for issues related to women, society does not tend to address it as a fight against women (unlike when women are the victim)

There have been thousands of cases of women being abused sexually in the form of rape, stalking, voyeurism, etc. In many societies, the woman will be the one blamed for her predicament and the man who committed the crime is allowed to go free.

These issues are not limited to sexual related harassment and crime but a systematic discrimination in schools, offices and political positions. In a world where women are more than men in population, you would expect to see more women occupying positions, but that is not the case even in high schools. Consider many organizations like soccer clubs, how many women have you seen coaching men football clubs?

CHAPTER FIVE

FINAL THOUGHTS

WE ALL SHOULD BE FEMINIST

According to Nelson Mandela "To deny people their human right is to challenge their very humanity"

For the society or any individual to restrict another human, to deprive them of that which naturally should be their right on the basis of their gender and not their skills or talent is disempowerment. When a society, community, organization approves of or accepts ideas, policies that deprive others, they stiffen talent, kill creativity and destroy destinies.

The feminist movement was born out of negative vices of oppression, violation, and deprivation of basic human rights. It is very possible to push people for a long period of time without getting a reaction from them, but the moment they are pushed to the wall, they would react in one form or the other. Feminism is a result of a certain gender (majorly women) being pushed to the wall.

True feminists acknowledge the fact that men and women are not the same physically and otherwise. However, they share similar rights as human beings and so deserve to have the same right of choice as the male gender.

The systematic deprivation in the political space and in organizations is obvious even to the blind. Inequality in salary scales still exists in some organizations, though progress has been made in past decades to bridge the gap.

In some societies, even to this day, the girl child is still considered unequal and of less value to the male child. This subtle accepted custom usually passed down from one generation to the next often corroborated by the help of the mothers and elderly women who have accepted the status quo is reflected in the choice of job, education, training and otherwise the female gender is allowed to access.

Feminism as a movement and activists in no small measures have made great progress across the world from corporations in the United States of America having women lead organizations and chair boards to Rwanda in Africa having over fifty percent lawmakers as women and to the local villages in Asian countries abolishing the old tradition that seem to place less value and importance to the girl or female child.

Feminism advocates for both male and female gender to enjoy their natural human rights. The cause is to fight injustice for the good of every human. Although the majority of the issues being addressed today are what the female gender goes through, there are very few cases of male gender rights being violated.

The door is open for all genders, the goal is to fight this injustice wherever it exists in our society.

In the words of Martin Luther King Junior, injustice anywhere is a threat to justice everywhere. Whatever affects one also affects others directly or indirectly. An organization that does not promote equality as a working culture will stiffen creativity and skills that could help boost their business and gain a competitive advantage.

No one, especially the female folk is completely immune to this violation. It could be your friend, wife, sister, brother, son, or even your daughter that may be a victim. If it is not happening in their home in form of abuse and they are forced not to speak about it, it could be in their place of work, and their professional career may be affected. This calls for the need for all to speak up!

"The ultimate tragedy is not the operation of bad people but the silence over that by good people"- Martin Luther King Jr.

It is high time we all as people with good conscience and the community at large rise up in one voice to fight against the vices of injustice on the basis of ones' gender.

It is on this backdrop that I call on all; men and women, ladies and gentlemen of good conscience especially the male gender to stand with women to fight and make the world a better place for all.